Magnetic: Master Likability Characteristics, Influence, and Instantly Learn How To Connect With
Others

Aiden Mccoy

© 2015

Disclaimer

Table of Contents

Introduction

Success requires hard work, skill, and talent... and one other thing: likability. Researchers have consistently found that likable people achieve more, and this is precisely because their charisma inspires others to support their endeavors. Fortunately, likability is not an esoteric branch of magic or a set of rare genes. It isn't founded on elusive concepts that are impossible to grasp with the intellectual mind, and it isn't a quality you can only possess if you were born with it. To the contrary, likability is a set of skills based on the science of psychology, and pretty much anyone can learn and use them.

According to researchers, likability leads to promotions, rewards, business success, the ability to close more sales and make more money, and the ability to get good service from waiters, doctors, and every other type of service provider. Non-likable people can get these things too, by intimidating, manipulating, or threatening others, but when someone *wants* to work with you, they do a much better job than they would if they *had* to work with you. They also enjoy their work more, which means they will continue to work with you rather than bailing out at the first opportunity.

In his 2007 article, "How to Become More Likable," Michael Lovas, an expert on the connection between psychology and professional credibility, tells us that likability is founded on verbal, facial, and vocal elements. Lovas asserts that the degree of sincerity in our facial expressions accounts for 55% of our likability—and for awkward moments like the one where you smile at a baby and it bursts into tears. The quality of our voice accounts for another 38% of likability. When you mirror the tone, pitch, and volume of the voice of the person you're talking to, they will perceive you as likable, whereas, if you shout, honk, squeak, or use an excessively nasal tone, you will repel them. The actual content of our speech accounts for a surprisingly low 7% of likability, and once again, in choosing words that mirror your audience's own values, you gain likability points.

Basically, people will like you if they feel like they know you, and they will feel like they know you if you appear to understand, relate to, and identify with them. In using facial expressions, words, and a tone of voice that mirror the person you're speaking to, you create an empathetic connection that makes them feel like you are on their side. If someone likes you and considers you an ally, they will trust you, and trust leads to productive working relationships and increased chances at success. In fact, according to Lovas, research shows that, in 83% of cases, the decision to work with someone was made based on likability, and people only do business with someone they don't like 17% of the time.

In order to project the sincerity necessary to inspire another person to like you, your facial expressions, vocal tone, and words must be consistent with your thought process. Say you're wearing a friendly smile, using an upbeat tone of voice, and telling someone, "That's a brilliant idea! Good job!" If, at the same time, you're thinking to yourself, "Oh, my god you are a completely useless moron," the person you're speaking to will perceive the inconsistency between your thoughts and your expressions, and it will make him or her uncomfortable and suspicious. Most people perceive such inconsistencies only on a subconscious level, but even so, the more inconsistent you are, the less people will trust you and like you and the less they will choose to work with you.

Basically, genuineness leads to likability, likability leads to trust, and trust leads to credibility, which is the one thing you need in order to be successful. While all three elements contribute to likability in differing degrees, each of them is equally essential. In switching either one of them off, you disable the other two as well. All three perceptual systems must working congruently with one another in order to project sincerity.

Lovas reminds us in his 2004 article, "Do People Like You?" that success in every aspect of business, including sales, seminars, management, hiring and recruiting, and dealing with brokers and dealers depends on likability. Mirroring the person or people you're speaking to during a sale or as you lead a seminar creates rapport, increases trust, and inspires devotion. Loyalty does more than make one sale, it creates a dedicated repeat customer. When it comes to hiring, recruiting, and management, likability enables you to assemble and effectively lead a group of individuals who are sincerely dedicated to your company's mission. If the success of your company depends on cultivating trusting relationships with brokers and dealers from other companies, likability could make or break you.

In his 2007 article, Lovas mentions a Stanford University study in which people were asked to rate the likability of 20 political figures on a scale from 1 to 100, with higher scores representing greater likability. Senator John Kerry ranked in the bottom three with a score of 39.6. Lovas points out that, while John Kerry projected confidence, his face always showed disdain and dislike. If people get the impression that you don't like them, they will not like you, hence Kerry's unsuccessful presidential campaign against the famously likable George W. Bush in 2004. Barack Obama, arguably one of the most likable politicians of recent times, ranked in the top three in that study, which was conducted around the time of his wildly successful 2008 presidential campaign.

Over the course of his career in psychology and finance, Lovas has concretely confirmed that we like people who remind us of ourselves. In crowds of strangers, we tend to gravitate toward those who walk, talk, dress, and look like us, down to the color of our hair and eyes. This is not discrimination. It stems from an ancient primordial survival tactic. From the earliest days of human kind, similarity has engendered trust. Even relationships that begin online are typically based on shared ideas, values, and physical traits.

Whether we like it or not, likability is essential to our success, not just in business, but in life. The world is full to the brim with people, and we will have to interact with them at some point in order to achieve our goals. People only help people whom they trust, and likability, because it demonstrates sincerity, understanding, and similarity, is the quality that builds that trust. Fortunately, likability can be learned and practiced, and subsequent chapters of this book will outline techniques for doing just that. It will also delve more deeply into how likability can be applied in various situations. Remember, likability is not manipulation, it is a quality you project when you align your thoughts and feelings with your voice, facial expressions, and words in order to portray authenticity.

Chapter 1: The Importance of Being Likable

You may be great at what you do. You may even be the best. And consistently doing great work will advance you up the ladder of success. But before you can climb that ladder, you need to secure the opportunity to demonstrate your abilities. No matter what your chosen career path, likability is the quality that will place you several rungs above other candidates when you interview for a position. A great resume and work history are essential, of course, but if you're competing against many others whose credentials and experience match or exceed your own, likability will be the determining factor in whether or not you win the job.

Likable people are easier to work with. Their personalities facilitate productive environments for collaboration and innovation. You may be a genius, but if no one wants to work with you, you become more of a hindrance than an asset for your employer. Rather than introduce friction into the workplace by hiring someone with a difficult personality, every sensible hiring manager will choose a more likable individual for the job. If a whole team can work productively together, they will probably accomplish just as much, if not more than one talented person who doesn't play well with others.

In opening up opportunities for us to demonstrate our abilities, likability leads to genuine praise from others, and this praise enhances our self-confidence. Many people believe that wit, cleverness, and physical attractiveness are the qualities that draw people to us, that win us friends and booming social lives. This is not the case. Physical attractiveness, wit, and cleverness can seem contrived if they do not come naturally to you and you try too hard to achieve them. Other people interpret these overt ploys for attention as a lack of genuineness, which ultimately drives them away rather than attracting them. It is self-confidence that really turns us into social magnates, and self-confidence comes naturally to us as a result of our achievements. Essentially, likability leads to opportunities for achievement, achievement leads to self-confidence, and self-confidence helps us build healthy relationships of all kinds.

In building healthy, trusting relationships, we become capable, productive leaders. The positive energy we radiate through likability and self-confidence creates an atmosphere of enthusiasm. It excites people and makes them want to be a part of what we are doing. In gaining the affinity, trust, and devotion of others, we establish conduits for effective communication. When people feel that you are their ally as well as their leader, and that your goal is to benefit everyone, they tend to endorse your ideas. Conversely, if people do not like and trust you, they will not believe that you care about them. They will suspect your motives and oppose your ideas at every opportunity. In inspiring others to endorse our ideas, we avoid wasting time and energy on constant disagreement, instead facilitating clear communication and an atmosphere of voluntary cooperation.

As leaders and innovators, we require space in which to maneuver. However, even leaders have bosses, and, like everyone else, we must secure the permission of our superiors before acting on our ideas. In addition to turning us into leaders in the first place, likability is the quality that gets us the permission and the resources we need to accomplish our goals. Using likability to get permission is not the same as engaging in the kinds of manipulation and deceit commonly used in office politics. Likability is based on a genuine intention to do great work and to help others do great work. It is inspired by the respect we show for others, the valuable contributions we make, the effective solutions we suggest when problems arise, and our willingness to not only work with others but also share the credit for a job well done. If our superiors find us likable, it is because they know that we intend to benefit everyone, not just ourselves, and this will inspire them to provide us with the resources we need.

It is rare than anyone, no matter how talented and capable, can accomplish great things alone. Every individual's success depends on help from others, and likability is the trait that will earn us their assistance. Thus the most effective method for increasing your own likability is to give others the credit and praise they deserve for their ideas, their contributions, and the time and effort they put into helping you achieve. In recognizing the talents and accomplishments of others, we help them find and harness their strengths, turning them into even more valuable members of the team. In this way, we increase the chances of success for ourselves, our colleagues, and the companies we work for.

Keep in mind that trying to become more likable does not make you some kind of selfish, egotistical narcissist. On the contrary, likability is important precisely because it empowers you to help everyone you meet develop their strengths and become more successful. The importance of being likable lies not solely in its ability to push an individual up the ladder of success, but in its ability to enable that individual to help others climb right alongside them.

Chapter 2: The Importance of Authenticity

In order to achieve the desired results, likability must be authentic. Authenticity is not a one-size fits all concept. In order to be authentic, you must become your best and truest self. No one is going to like you if you go through life mimicking the mannerisms, traits, and qualities of the successful individuals you admire. In trying to be someone other than yourself, you are being dishonest. When people sense dishonesty, they suspect your motives and choose to steer clear of you. Instead, you must discover your own best qualities and traits, and use your own natural mannerisms to display and enhance them. You must find your own strengths and talents, and you must use them. In doing so, you hone them to perfection, giving yourself the confidence to achieve *your goals, your way.*

Authenticity empowers you to take control of your own life. In forcing ourselves to behave in certain ways because we think others want us to, we make puppets of ourselves.

We allow outside influence to pull the strings that direct every aspect of our lives. We wear what we're told to wear, we smile when people tell us to smile—regardless of whether or not we feel good, and we choose careers and life paths that satisfy everyone except ourselves. As a puppet, you feel small, helpless, and ineffective. You feel like you have no control over your own life. When you choose to become your true, authentic self, you begin to take direction from within, and following those instructions feels much more natural. In becoming the you that you are meant to be, you transfer power to yourself, and people are attracted to powerful people who appear to be in control.

The first step to becoming your authentic self is to examine every aspect of your life and ask yourself if your current situation reflects your true desires. Ask yourself if your relationships are based on mutual respect or if they are based on a desire for personal gain. Ask yourself if you really love your job or if you chose it in order to satisfy someone else's expectations. Do your spiritual practices actually fulfill and inspire you, or are you going through the motions in order to comply with tradition? The purpose of this in-depth self-examination is to discover whether your desires come from within you, or if they are superimposed on you by others under the guise of cultural norms. If you are pursuing a life path that is not cohesive with your true nature, you will never achieve the authenticity necessary for likability.

If in-depth self-examination leads you to the conclusion that you are not on the right path, don't be discouraged, there is a way to find it. All you have to do is follow your passions. What are you good at? What do you love to do? It doesn't matter if your true passions seem impractical. What's important is that they come from within, that they are not the products of outside influence. Passions that come from within are powered by our true nature, our authentic selves. They inspire the excitement and enthusiasm necessary to keep us focused, dedicated, and determined so that we can translate them into something practical.

Don't worry, you don't have to change your life overnight. You can follow your passions one small step at a time, and with every step, you will become more authentic. For example, say you've always wanted to be a writer. Start by enrolling yourself in a journalism course or a creative writing class at the local community college. The class will give you a structured way to integrate your passion into your busy schedule. Learning the basics will inspire you to delve deeper into the subject and become more advanced. You'll make connections with your teacher and other students, and these relationships will open doors to opportunities. They will also offer support and inspiration if ever you doubt your chosen path.

The skills and knowledge you gain as you begin learning about your subject of passion will increase your self-confidence, and using those skills will make you happier. You will begin to radiate positivity, and it will draw others to you. Your excitement will build with every inch of progress, and because real excitement is contagious, you will notice positive changes in your personal interactions. You won't have to ask people to help you out. They will want to support you in your endeavors, and you will have the drive and desire to support them in return. A shared enthusiasm for the work at hand will enable good communication and a productive working atmosphere, which will ultimately lead to achievement and further opportunity. In following your passions, you become your true self, and that authenticity naturally brings forth all of the qualities that make up likability, thus empowering you to bring about success for yourself and others.

However, once you've established true authenticity, you must make a concerted effort to stay true to yourself. Maintaining authenticity will become much more difficult once you have tasted success. The praise and admiration you receive as a result of your achievements will make you want to reach ever higher, but if you become addicted to that outside validation, you risk putting yourself in a negative position. Rather than working for the love of what you do, you will begin to work for praise and glory. You will begin to do whatever you have to do in order to gain the approval of others. You will find yourself right back where you started—living an inauthentic life that is dictated to you via outside influence.

It is of utmost importance that you remember where your success really came from. True success never comes from outside, it comes from inside. It was not given to you by those who now praise and admire you. You earned it by following your true passions and working to become your authentic self. If you continue to follow your true life path, your enthusiasm and drive will never fail and you will continue to accomplish one goal after another.

If you do find yourself losing interest or inspiration, repeat the self-examination process mentioned earlier in this chapter. If, in doing so, you come to the conclusion that you are once again truly unhappy, change course. It is not necessary to choose one path and stick with it forever. For some people, even the true life path branches off into new territory occasionally. Life is evolution. We walk one road until we've soaked up its wisdom, then we turn a corner or take a fork in order to discover new wisdom. In this way, we add depth and dimension to our authentic selves. Our core identity doesn't change, it builds and becomes more complete.

In re-evaluating your life every time you lose your drive, you ensure that you never miss a turn on your path to personal evolution. By following your passions, even when they change dramatically, you become a more complete version of your authentic self, and in doing so, you maintain the positive attributes that make up likability and lead to success.

It is easier to maintain drive, enthusiasm, and productivity when you are working and striving from a place of authenticity. Being yourself comes naturally once you figure out what your true self really is. On the other hand, trying to be something you're not eats up a lot of energy that you could be using to accomplish your goals. Because authenticity is easier to maintain than a contrived personality, we are more likely to be consistent in our personalities, our work habits, and our personal relationships when we are being our true selves, and consistency is the essence of integrity.

Integrity is the most important trait or quality a person can possess when it comes to forming relationships of any kind, whether personal or business-related. It tells people they can trust you and depend on you. If people always know what to expect from you, they'll feel much more comfortable around you, and they will come to you for answers and leadership. This opens up further opportunities for advancement.

The most important thing to remember about the relationship between authenticity and likability is that, in living as your authentic self, you invite success, and with every success, you will *like yourself* a little more. Genuinely liking yourself is not the same as harboring a massive ego. It does not mean that you think you are better than others, it simply means that you are perfectly comfortable with who you are. When it comes down to it, the real key to becoming likable is to *like yourself,* and it is authenticity that will enable you to achieve this vital first step. Once you have found authenticity, everything else will follow.

Chapter 3: Likability in Conversation

Nowhere is likability more important than in conversation. As previously discussed, conversation opens the doors to opportunity. Only when those doors have opened can we demonstrate our true worth to others. This doesn't just apply in business situations, it applies when forming friendships, romantic relationships, and human connections of every other kind. Because there are no second chances at first impressions, the first conversation you have with every person you meet will likely determine how they feel about you right then and forever more. Don't get too nervous. Although likability is essential to the good conversation upon which healthy, productive relationships are based, achieving it may be easier than you think.

The first thing you need to know is that people like talking about themselves. According to Diana Tamir, a neuroscientist at Harvard, talking about ourselves pleases us as much as receiving money or consuming food. One of the best ways to start a conversation is to ask a person how things have been going in their life. You can further enhance the other person's enjoyment of the conversation by appearing interested, which you can do by maintaining eye contact, summing up what they've told you, and asking questions that will encourage further disclosure.

While initial conversations are most important, those in which someone asks for your input can have an equally weighty effect on a relationship. A person sharing what they think is a great idea, or even just asking for an opinion on a new dress is putting themselves in a vulnerable position. This vulnerability adds weight to anything you might say in response. When someone asks you for feedback on an idea and you detect gaps in their reasoning, don't just tell them it's a bad idea. Instead, lead them to insights that will help them improve the idea. You can do this by asking questions that will encourage the person to explain each aspect of their idea and give them the opportunity to spot the gaps. This is a much less threatening approach to giving feedback. It allows the person to feel that they have arrived at a solution on their own. Empowering people to exercise their own problem-solving abilities definitely makes you more likable.

Another way to earn affinity is to ask people for advice. This tactic enables you to influence others even when you lack authority on the subject at hand. Because asking for advice creates an atmosphere of sharing and collaboration, it works well in confrontational situations such as negotiations. In asking the other person to contribute their knowledge, you imply that their experience and wisdom are valuable. In making the other person feel intelligent and valued, you give them the impression that you are their ally rather than their opposition. Showing people that you want to work *with* them and help them get what they need significantly increases your likability.

One of the most powerful ways to increase your likability is to make people feel better about their own lives. This tactic works especially well in situations that require you to bring up unpleasant topics that might otherwise make for a negative conversational experience. Begin by asking the person a question about an aspect of their life that you happen to know is going well. Once they've answered, feel free to bring up the less appealing subject. In encouraging the person to talk about something positive, you improve their overall mood, and this improvement carries over into the rest of the conversation, also improving the person's outlook on the more negative subject. Making people feel better about their problems is an extremely effective method for enhancing likability.

Perhaps the simplest approach to creating likability in conversation is a technique known as *active listening*. When your conversation partner pauses, repeat the last two or three words of what he or she said, adding a question inflection to your voice. This lets the person know that you have been listening, that you are interested, and that you want to hear more. In conveying these three things to another person, you add value to what they're saying, thereby increasing their self-worth, and who doesn't like a person that can make them feel more valued? As long as you're careful not to come off like a parrot, and as long as your tone is never mocking, this technique will always work.

Another way to increase likability is to speak positively about others—whether they are present or not. Research shows that what you say about others affects how people perceive you. If you say positive things about other people, they will perceive you as pleasant. If you say negative things, people will perceive you as unpleasant. If you regularly complain about someone else's incompetence, for instance, the people to whom you make your complaints will associate you with that incompetence to the point that they begin to apply that negative trait to you. Instead, look for things a person does well, compliment them, and talk about those positive traits to others when that person is absent. If you do this regularly, people will begin to attach to you the positive traits you talk about. As a bonus, consciously searching for the good in others improves our outlook on life in general, and the resulting increase in positivity makes you even more likable.

Likability in conversation leads to likability in general, and achieving it is relatively simple. All you have to do is take an interest in the other person. Show them that you're listening and that you value what they have to say. Make sure they know that you're willing to work *with* them even in confrontational situations, and encourage them to discover their own solutions to problems. Most importantly, always speak positively about others, and always encourage them to embrace the most positive possible perspective of their own lives. No matter what the situation or the subject at hand, remembering even one off the above techniques during your next conversation will improve your chances at making a good impression and gaining the trust and affinity of the person with whom you're speaking.

Chapter 4: Likability & Relationship Building

Productive business relationships are not the only human connections that contribute to our happiness and satisfaction. Even the most introverted among us has an innate need to form intimate personal connections with other people. We all need friends, family, and romantic love. We all need to feel like we belong in a group or a pairing. Because exclusion and social rejection lead to depression, anxiety, and other serious psychological disturbances, we're all highly motivated to connect with other people on various levels.

Likability is crucial to forming everything from casual friendships and acquaintances to spousal and parental bonds. Unfortunately, there is a severe disconnect between what most of us think are likable traits and what most of us *actually like*. In his Huffington Post article, "What Makes a Person Likeable?" psychologist Roger Covin, Ph.D., tells us that, when asked what their most likable traits are, people tend to list physical appearance, income, and social status. However, when asked what they want in a friend or romantic partner, they list qualities like kindness, loyalty, honesty, and trustworthiness.

Covin attributes this disconnect to cultural conditioning. Through guidance from our caregivers, spiritual practices, and life experience, we learn the value of qualities like honesty and trustworthiness, but modern western culture contradicts those values with its relentless celebration of superficial attributes such as expensive material possessions, outer beauty, fame, and money. We are endlessly barraged by advertisements assuring us that material possessions and the use of beauty products will bring us acceptance and love.

Pointing to a study performed in the 1960s by psychologist Norman Anderson, in which Anderson asked people to rate 555 words according to the degree to which they would make a person likable, Covin affirms that qualities like sincerity, honesty, and a capacity for understanding were indeed the most likable human traits. Humor and intelligence also neared the top of the list, while popularity ranked significantly lower.

Of course, the qualities we desire in a casual same-sex friend will differ from those we expect in our spouse. Covin emphasizes the importance of a more recent study, in which psychologists established five different relationship categories and asked participants to rate 16 qualities according to how much they desired them in a given type of relationship. The relationship categories were as follows: same-sex friends, opposite-sex friends, dating partners, marriage partners, and casual sex partners. Remarkably, though they appeared in a different order for each relationship type, the top three most desired qualities for all five categories were warmth and kindness, openness and expressiveness, and sense of humor. For most categories, superficial attributes like beauty and wealth rated 8th or lower.

Covin concludes, based on his own experience as a psychologist and on decades worth of research, that when it comes to being likable in any type of relationship, the traits that make up a good personality are far more important than material wealth, social status, and physical attractiveness. These are more like bonus traits. They increase likability, but they don't define it.

It's easy to understand why kindness, openness, humor, and understanding are so desirable, but in delving more deeply into Norman Anderson's list of 555 traits, we gain a more comprehensive understanding of the ways in which we could refine our personalities in order to increase likability. For example, being critical, vulgar, jealous, or prejudiced would rank you extremely low on the list. This seems rather obvious, but we must keep in mind that no person can claim to be immune to jealousy, and none of us can say we've never criticized anyone. There are certain very undesirable traits that all of us exhibit to some degree, and it is very hard to gauge just how often we do so.

It is important to develop and awareness of our own behavior in an effort to avoid being overly critical or stiflingly jealous, as these traits in particular can wear a friend or romantic partner down and cause them to lose interest in us over time. If someone tells you that you're being too jealous or too critical, try not to get defensive. This will only exacerbate the other person's discomfort. Instead, try recalling your recent interactions with that person. Search for moments in which you did indeed exhibit those negative behaviors. Try to picture ways in which you could have acted more positively.

In addition to monitoring our own behavior, it is important to pay close attention to the personality traits of others. Remember, people tend to like those who are similar to themselves, which is why mirroring has such a profound effect on attraction. We can use it to determine what gestures, words, and tones of voice to use in conversation, and it applies to personal relationships as well as business connections. For instance, a recent study conducted by Justin Harris Moss of University of North Carolina

Wilmington, concluded that mirroring someone's style of humor increases sexual attraction. Interestingly, Harris also found that self-defeating humor is more attractive than self-enhancing humor. Egotism ranked very low on Anderson's list of personality traits, so it follows that an ability to make light of ourselves would also be a likable quality.

The ability to form healthy personal relationships is essential to our psychological well-being, and likability is our most effective tool for initiating them. Knowing the difference between pop culture's definition of likable and our innate human definition of likable is the key to attracting friends and romantic partners. Remember, your good personality traits are far more valuable than physical appearance, popularity, or material wealth. In noticing the effects our more negative traits have on others and adjusting them accordingly, and in mirroring the good qualities of the person we want to attract, we move ourselves up rung by rung on the likability scale, significantly increasing our chances at forming healthy personal relationships that will improve our overall quality of life.

Chapter 5: 20 Traits, Habits, & Qualities Shared by Likable People

Now that you have a general understanding of what likability is and how it can be used to form healthy, productive relationships, let's get more specific. Here is a list of traits, qualities, and habits that likable people apply across situations of all types during their daily lives. Read them over, compare them to your own behaviors, and consider how you might begin to integrate them into your daily interactions with others. Begin with your favorite one and focus exclusively on it until you feel it's become second nature, then move through the list one at a time. You will find that with time and practice, likability can be learned, mastered and used to manifest success and happiness.

Choose a Positive Mindset: It is much easier to be a cynic than it is to maintain positivity in the face of the constant challenges of daily life, but remember, you *choose* your attitude and your perspective. When you interact with others, they will sense your optimism and determination.

Use a Confident Tone of Voice: Confident does not mean forceful or aggressive. It means speaking in even tones that mirror those of the person you're talking to, and it means choosing your words with intent and precision.

Listen: Don't forget that we human beings find it enormously pleasing to talk about ourselves. Ask people questions about their lives, listen carefully, and repeat a few words of what they say in order to indicate that you're paying attention.

Focus: This one goes hand in hand with listening. During conversations, you must pay exclusive and constant attention to the person who is speaking. This doesn't mean staring them straight in the eyes throughout the conversation, it just means that you should put your phone away, avoid glancing at the television playing CNN in the corner, and stop looking at the clock. If you allow little things to distract you from the conversation, the person speaking will think that you don't care what they have to say.

Don't Overreact: Maintaining a calm, even demeanor in every situation, no matter how aggravating, is more likable than displaying anger. It gives people the impression that you are in control and that they can depend on you to lead them to a solution. Anger, on the other hand, sets people on edge and makes people want to avoid you.

Be Genuine: Genuineness earns you the trust of others. If it seems as though you're trying to be something you're not, people will suspect you and your intentions. Instead, follow your passions toward a life path that satisfies the true you. This will make you happier and draw others to you.

Be Patient: The way you time your speech and actions has an incredible impact on how comfortable people feel around you, and on whether or not you appear to value them and what they have to say. Don't interrupt others and don't be too eager to lecture them about your own opinions or ideas. Listen first, then look for the best possible moment to speak.

Be Open-minded: Listening to and genuinely considering the ideas and perspectives of others leads to personal growth and it makes you seem more receptive and innovative. On the other hand, only associating with people who think like you is not just limiting, it is extremely frustrating for those who must work with you.

Smile: This one may seem obvious and even trite, but it works. A smile—one that involves the whole face, not just the mouth—is disarming. It makes people feel they can trust you. It also gives the impression that you enjoy what you're doing, which makes people want to work with you and support your efforts.

Express Yourself Selectively: We all wish we could speak aloud every thought that enters our minds. We all think that every single one of our opinions and ideas are valuable. But in expressing every single thought that crosses your mind, you monopolize conversations and waste time on irrelevant—or worse, offensive—comments. Before you speak, thoroughly consider whether or not what you have to say will move the conversation forward in a productive way.

Avoid Procrastination: Repeatedly putting off your responsibilities until the last possible second shows others that you are afraid of failure and that you are lazy, which together give the impression that you are ineffective. It also causes the people you work with to have to constantly worry about whether or not you'll finally get your work done. Because your work likely affects the progress of someone else's work, procrastinating causes other people undue stress. Conversely, being proactive significantly increases likability.

Be Generous: This means with your time, your skill, and your knowledge. When someone needs help, lend a hand, and most importantly, do no expect anything in return. Generosity is much more likable than putting others in debt to you. When people know they can come to you for help without having to worry about "paying you back," you become one of the most likable people around.

Learn from Your Failures: Our mistakes and mishaps often leave us with valuable wisdom we could not have learned any other way. In actively looking for this wisdom and applying it to your life, you inspire others. On the other hand, if you wallow in your failures, allowing them to stop you in your tracks, others will perceive you as weak.

Learn About Others: One of the best ways to become more likable is to take an interest in other people. Use conversations as opportunities to learn about their lives, their goals, and their passions and interests. Let them speak and continue to ask questions. While everyone wants to be known and understood, some are less comfortable revealing themselves. They have to be drawn gently out of their shells. In becoming the type of person who makes an effort to get to know even those who don't make it easy, you show that you really care about other people.

Praise Others: This one is very important, but it must not be overdone. Give people credit where credit is due. Recognize their achievements. Compliment people on their work, their skills, and their knowledge. Just don't go around lavishing flattery on everyone in sight as this will not be perceived as genuine.

Welcome Honest Feedback: The most important thing to realize about being likable is that pretending does not work. You must genuinely care about your conduct and your reputation. To find out if you're approaching your goals in the best possible way, ask a trusted confidant for his or her thoughts on your behavior and actions. Make sure you ask someone who is honest and who knows you well, and make sure you hear them out and apply their advice.

Don't Judge: If people get the feeling that you've formed an unchangeable impression of them before you've even attempted to get to know them, they will steer clear of you. Instead of judging people based on their appearance or what you heard about them from someone else, make an effort to find out what kind of person they truly are. It is also important to avoid trying to change people. In allowing people to be who they are, you make people feel a lot more comfortable around you.

Shift the Focus to Others: People are generally repelled by those who seem too desperate for attention. Remember, you don't have to suddenly become an outgoing, over-the-top extrovert in order to attract the attention and gain the affinity of others. Just be yourself and pay attention to people when they speak. And when you do accomplish something great, make sure to shift the praise onto those who helped you. In making others feel appreciated, you gain more respect for your achievements.

Be a Mirror, Not a Manipulator: Remember that people feel a lot more comfortable around those who resemble themselves. Instead of coercing people to work *for* you under threat of punishment, inspire them to work *with* you by making them feel that you are their ally. This can be accomplished by mirroring a person's tone of voice, sense of humor, or facial expressions.

Be Consistent: Consistency may be the most important trait shared by likable people. People need to feel like they can depend on you, and if your mood, personality, and work habits shift constantly, making it impossible for people to rely on you, they will avoid you altogether. Consistency comes from being yourself and from not allowing your personal life to affect your work life—or the other way around.

Because it's so difficult to view ourselves objectively, it can be hard to know where to begin when attempting to learn and master likability. A good first step would be to ask people who know you well to tell you which of the above traits you need to work on. Ask them to be totally honest, and encourage future honesty by refraining from getting defensive. Thank them for being forthright and use their advice to begin your transformation into a more authentic, more likable version of yourself.

Conclusion

We all want to be successful and live up to our fullest potential, and likability is the only quality which, all on its own, can empower us to accomplish all of our personal and business-related goals. When combined with hard work, skill, and talent, likability will never fail to inspire others to support us in our endeavors. Likability is the essence of effective leadership, and it creates opportunities for innovation that will advance us and those we work with up the ladder of success. Likability is a multi-dimensional quality, a set of skills, which, fortunately, can be learned and mastered by anyone.

The skills necessary to increase your own likability are all based on one foundational concept: people like people who appear to be like them. As long as you keep this idea in mind and allow it to direct all of your behaviors, you will give others the impression that you understand and relate to them—that you are their ally. When people feel that they know you and that you know them, they trust you and like you.

You may be trying to get a date with the man or woman of your dreams, or you may be interviewing for your dream job. In either case, you will be competing with others who may be as qualified, or maybe even more qualified for the position than you. Likability is of utmost importance because it is the quality that will set you above your competition. The reality is, no matter what the situation, and no matter how talented or attractive you are, the individual making the choice will always choose the person who is easiest to work with, and it is likability that makes you easy to work with.

Because likability opens the doors to opportunity, and by extension, the doors to accomplishment, it leads to an increase in self-confidence. It is self-confidence that earns us the trust and devotion of others. It inspires them to endorse our ideas and work with us, turning us into strong leaders. Effective leadership and support from others leads to cooperation and good communication, which are the essential elements of a productive working atmosphere. In using likability to become a strong leader, you benefit others as well as yourself, helping them develop their strengths and make valuable contributions that lead to success for everyone.

Remember that the key to increasing your likability is to become your authentic self. In doing so, you cease to be an ineffectual puppet whose life is dictated by outside influence. You empower yourself to take control of your own life. Authenticity is not hard to achieve. All you have to do is follow your true passions. They will set you on a life path that will lead to happiness, satisfaction, and contagious enthusiasm that will make others want to work with you. Just remember to make a conscious effort to stay true to yourself once you become successful. Always work for the love of what you do, not for praise and glory, otherwise you risk turning yourself back into a puppet controlled by the desire for outside validation. Also, keep in mind that your true life path may branch or fork at some point, and that in following it you add depth and dimension to your life and evolve into a more complete version of your authentic self. Authenticity helps you *like yourself*, which will inspire others to like you too.

Authenticity will also help you make excellent first impressions and become a good conversationalist, and success in every type of human relationship is founded on positive communication. Start by asking people questions and allowing them to talk about themselves. If someone asks you for feedback on an idea, ask questions that will lead them to insights and allow them to find their own solutions. Empowering others to solve problems significantly increases your likability. Also, ask for input and advice from others in order to create a collaborative atmosphere and minimize confrontation. Keep in mind that the most effective way to enhance likability is to make others feel good about their lives—even the more negative aspects of it—by encouraging them to think and talk about positive things. Speaking of positivity, remember to find the good qualities in others. Talking about another person's better traits improves your outlook on life and causes others to think of you in positive ways.

Likability is essential to forming relationships of all kinds. Remember that the traits that make up a good personality, such as honesty and a sense of humor, are far more important than the more superficial traits promoted through the media. Take no heed of the advertisements that tell you over and over again that material possessions and beauty products will bring you acceptance and love. They do not have your best interests in mind, they just want your money. Instead, remember that, no matter what type of relationship you're pursuing, kindness, honesty, and trustworthiness will remain the most desired traits. When it comes to managing those negative traits we all share, make an effort to listen to people you care about and use their observations to refine your behavior. Remember that forming healthy personal relationships is essential your mental well-being and that likability will help you initiate and maintain them.

Becoming more likable will significantly improve your quality of life. Authenticity, positivity, passion, and good communication skills are essential to likability. Don't let the loftiness of all those concepts overwhelm you. Just remember that likability boils down to one concept: people like people who are like themselves. To gain trust from others, show them that you understand, value, and identify with them. There are plenty of tactics and techniques you can use to gain trust and affinity. Start with the ones listed in the previous chapter of this book. Move gradually through the list, and almost immediately you will notice a distinct improvement in your relationships, your self-confidence, and your ability to accomplish your goals and manifest your dreams.

www.ingramcontent.com/pod-product-compliance
Lightning Source LLC
Chambersburg PA
CBHW070825290526
45795CB00002B/841